PREHISTORIC OCEANS

by Dougal Dixon

NEW
FOREST
PRESS

CONTENTS

Publisher: Tim Cook
Editor: Guy Croton
Designer: Carol Davis
Production Controller: Ed Green
Production Manager: Suzy Kelly

ISBN: 978-1-84898-332-8
Library of Congress Control Number: 2010925200
Tracking number: nfp0006

North American edition copyright
© TickTock Entertainment Ltd. 2010
First published in North America in 2010 by
New Forest Press, PO Box 784, Mankato, MN 56002
www.newforestpress.com

Printed in the USA
9 8 7 6 5 4 3 2 1

Every effort has been made to trace the copyright
holders, and we apologize in advance for any
omissions. We would be pleased to insert the
appropriate acknowledgments in any subsequent
edition of this publication.

The author has asserted his right to be identified
as the author of this book in accordance with the
Copyright, Design, and Patents Act, 1988.

PREHISTORIC OCEANS

INTRODUCTION

Sea monsters! The dread of every medieval sailor questing into the unknown. The goal of every cryptozoologist, looking for animals new to science. The ocean abounds with huge animals—whales, sharks, giant squid. Who knows what else might be lurking out there in the depths? But the great sea beasts of today, fascinating though they are, are more than matched by the fabulous array of marine creatures that have come and gone throughout the history of the earth.

Fossil sea creatures have long been known to us. The fossils of animals that lived in the ocean have always been much more common than fossils of animals that lived on land. We can see why. An animal that dies on land lies on the ground. It is torn apart and scattered by scavenging animals, and the flesh is eaten by carrion-eating birds. Then its bones rot in the weather, or may be consumed by insects. Soon all that is left of the animal is a smear on the ground—nothing to fossilize.

In the sea a dead animal will sink to the bottom. There it may be covered by mud or sand before it has a chance to be eaten by scavengers. Then, as the mud and sand eventually turn to rock, the remains of the animal are turned to mineral and its bones become fossilized.

That is why scientists knew about fossil sea animals long before they knew about fossil land-living dinosaurs.

Life first evolved in the sea, and it was only in Silurian times that it first ventured out on to land. Of course the vast majority of sea-living organisms are those whose ancestors never left the sea in the first place, and have continued to evolve as the seas themselves have evolved. Amongst the vertebrates these are the creatures that we call the fish. But the bigger vertebrates are those that turned their backs on the land-living existence and returned to their ancestral home—the oceans. This is quite in keeping with all the other big patterns of evolution. If there is a lifestyle to be lived, a niche to be occupied, a resource to be exploited, evolution will allow the development of something that will take advantage.

So, in the age of reptiles, we find reptiles abandoning life on land and taking to a marine lifestyle. There were the turtles, and these are still with us. There were the elasmosaurs, with turtle-like bodies, long necks, and short heads. There were the closely related pliosaurs, with short necks and long heads. There were giant sea lizards called mosasaurs. And there were the best-adapted of all aquatic reptiles, the ichthyosaurs, with their streamlined bodies and fish-like fins. Then when these were wiped away at the end of the Cretaceous period their places were taken by mammals that followed the same course. Along came the whales and dolphins, the seals and sea lions, the dugongs and manatees—all with their particular adaptations to the aquatic way of life.

And we can plot all this in the fossil record. Everywhere that there are sedimentary rocks that originated at the bottom of the ocean, we have a chance of finding fossils of the animals that lived there. The constant movement of the continents of the earth's crust mean that sediments that once lay on the shallow continental shelves or the ocean depths, may now be found outcropping in mountainous areas, or in cliffs by the beach. Natural history museums throughout the world have their collections of fossil sea animals, collected locally or brought in from other areas. Sometimes they are displayed still in the block of rock in which they were found—often the preservation is so good that the whole skeleton lies there undisturbed. Sometimes the bones have been extracted, prepared and mounted in lifelike poses, as is often done with dinosaur skeletons.

There is so much that we know about the extinct sea animals, but there is still so much to be discovered. It is an evolving science.

THE FIRST SWIMMERS

All life came from the sea. Scientists estimate that life appeared 3.5 billion years ago and that plants and animals only relatively recently came out on to land (about 400 million years ago for plants and 300 million years ago for animals). Some of the first land creatures evolved into reptiles and dinosaurs. But the ways of evolution are complex. Almost as soon as life on land was established, some life forms returned to the sea to exploit new food sources. As early as 250 million years ago, water-living animals had evidently evolved from land-living ancestors.

A MODERN EXAMPLE

The Galapagos marine iguana, which looks and lives very much like some of the early swimming reptiles, has adopted a partially aquatic way of life because it feeds on seaweed. Its lizard body, legs, and feet show that it is a land-living animal, but its muscular, flexible tail is ideal for swimming. It also can hold its breath for long periods, and it can remove from its system excess salt absorbed from seawater. These are adaptations that fail to show up on fossil animals, so we do not know if early swimming reptiles had them.

THE BUOYANCY PROBLEM

Hovasaurus, from Upper Permian rocks found in Madagascar, had a swimming tail twice the length of its body. Although this tail was so long that it would have been difficult to use on land, its feet were those of a land-living reptile. Most skeletons of *Hovasaurus* have pebbles in the stomach area. Evidently *Hovasaurus* swallowed stones to adjust its buoyancy underwater. This swimming technique was used by animals whose ancestors were land-living animals (*see page 14*).

CARBONIFEROUS 354-290 MYA	PERMIAN 290-248 MYA	TRIASSIC 248-206 MYA	EARLY/MID JURASSIC 206-159 MYA	LATE JURASSIC 159-144 MYA

A RETRO-PIONEER

Spinoaequalis, the earliest-known land animal to return to a water-living existence, was a lizardlike beast found in Upper Carboniferous marine sediments in Kansas. Its name means "equal spine," which refers to the strong spines on the tail that made a flat vertical paddle to which strong muscles were attached. This is the tail of a swimming animal. The rest of the skeleton is that of a land-living creature.

A FRESHWATER PUZZLE

Mesosaurus was a freshwater reptile, about 3 feet (1 meter) long, with a flattened swimming tail and powerful webbed hind legs. It probably used its tail and hind legs to drive itself through the water and steered and stabilized itself with its webbed front feet. Its teeth were fine and needle-like and were probably used for filtering invertebrates from the water to eat. The odd thing about it, though, is the fact that its skeletons are found in Lower Permian rocks in both South Africa and Brazil. Scientists wondered how the remains of a freshwater animal were fossilized on two widely separated continents. It was the first piece of evidence in support of a revolutionary concept called "plate tectonics."

ABOUT PLATE TECTONICS

In Permian times, when *Mesosaurus* was alive, there was no Atlantic Ocean. What is now Africa and South America were part of a single vast landmass called Pangaea. The same kinds of animals lived all over the world because there were no oceans to separate them. The presence of the skeleton of *Mesosaurus* in South Africa and Brazil was one of the first pieces of evidence supporting the theory of continental drift—now better known as "plate tectonics."

AN ECOLOGICAL OVERVIEW

The prehistoric seas and oceans were full of life and supported complex food chains. At the bottom of the food chain were the algae, growing and reproducing by absorbing energy from the Sun and taking nutrition from the water. Filter-feeding animals like mollusks fed on these and in turn were preyed upon by fish and other vertebrates. Higher up the chain, these creatures were threatened by even bigger invertebrates that were themselves foodstuff for the largest and most powerful of the sea animals. When any of these animals died, their decaying bodies provided nutrition in the seawater, allowing the algae to grow. The links in this process produced a cycle of life, death, decay, and new life.

THE CRETACEOUS SEAS

The shallow seas of the Late Cretaceous (such as those that covered central North America) were filled with ammonites. By this time, the ammonites were not just free-floating and actively hunting ammonites; they also included drifting, filter-feeding forms, and crawling types, such as giant snails, that fed on the seabed. The fish-hunters of the shallow waters were the mosasaurs, while out to sea lived the elasmosaurs and the giant pliosaurs. Pterosaurs still fished from the sky, but they were now joined by the creatures that were to be their successors—the birds.

SEA CROCODILES

THE TRIASSIC SEAS

Shellfish on the shallow floor of the Triassic seas were eaten by slow-moving placodonts. Fish were chased by nothosaurs, which were precursors of the plesiosaurs. Long-bodied ichthyosaurs also chased the fish and the ammonites (a prehistoric mollusk) of the time. We are still not sure where the giant ichthyosaurs fit into this pattern. They were probably fish eaters and ammonite eaters as well, and they could hunt in deep water.

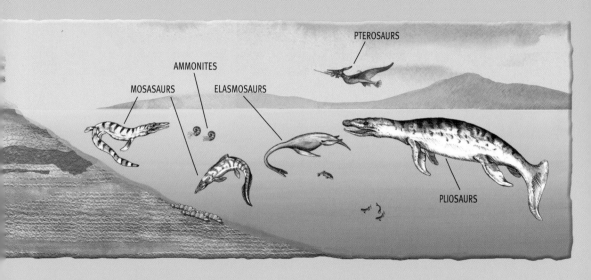

ILS

PTEROSAURS

AMMONITES

MOSASAURS   ELASMOSAURS

PLIOSAURS

THE JURASSIC SEAS

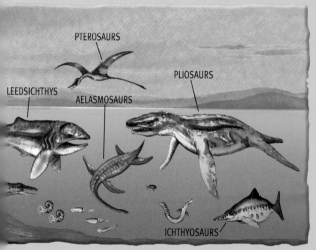

PTEROSAURS

LEEDSICHTHYS   PLIOSAURS

AELASMOSAURS

ICHTHYOSAURS

The shallow seas that covered much of what is today northern Europe were bountiful in Jurassic times, supporting many different kinds of animals. One of these was *Leedsichthys*, a giant filter-feeding fish that must have lived and fed like a modern basking shark. In shallow waters lived sea crocodiles, which fed on the fish of the area. The fish and ammonites of the deeper waters were hunted by ichthyosaurs, while closer to the surface they were hunted by elasmosaurs, which were, in turn, hunted by the great pliosaurs. Dipping into the waves to fish were the flying reptiles, the pterosaurs.

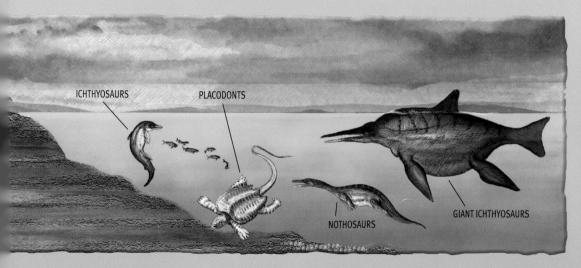

ICHTHYOSAURS   PLACODONTS

GIANT ICHTHYOSAURS

NOTHOSAURS

A SHOAL OF SWIMMING REPTILES

We have a good record of water-living animals because in an environment where sediment is constantly accumulating, these creatures have a better chance of being fossilized. From these fossils, we know that many of the sea creatures were in fact reptiles that had left dry land for a new life in the water. If there was more food in the water than on land, and if there were fewer dangerous predators in the sea, an aquatic life would have become enticing. Reptiles can adapt quite easily to such a lifestyle. They have a low metabolic rate and they can cope without oxygen for some time. In addition, moving around in the water takes only about a quarter of the energy of moving about on land.

A MODERN TURTLE

The turtle is a slow-moving aquatic reptile, shelled above and below, with paddle limbs that allow it to move through the water with a flying action. Protected from its enemies and surrounded by sources of food, it does not need speed or a streamlined shape to thrive.

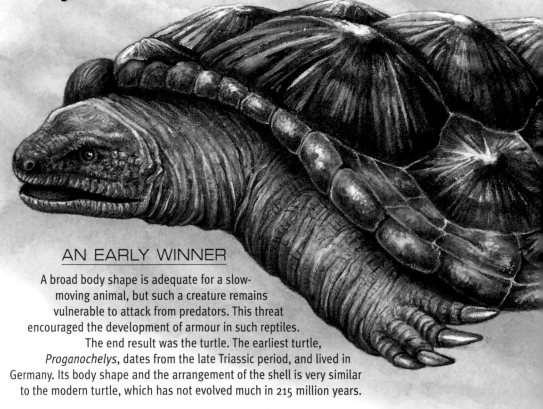

AN EARLY WINNER

A broad body shape is adequate for a slow-moving animal, but such a creature remains vulnerable to attack from predators. This threat encouraged the development of armour in such reptiles. The end result was the turtle. The earliest turtle, *Proganochelys*, dates from the late Triassic period, and lived in Germany. Its body shape and the arrangement of the shell is very similar to the modern turtle, which has not evolved much in 215 million years.

LIFE AFTER DEATH

The science of taphonomy deals with what happens to an animal after it dies and how it becomes a fossil. Here is how this process occurs at sea.

1. When an animal dies, it may float on the surface for a while until the gases generated in its decaying tissues disperse.

2. Eventually, it sinks to the bottom of the sea. A less buoyant animal may go straight to the bottom. There it may be scavenged by bottom-living creatures, its parts broken up and dispersed.

3. If sand and mud are being deposited rapidly on the seabed, the body is quickly buried before too much damage is done.

4. After millions of years, the sand and mud will be compressed and cemented together as rock, and the bones of the dead animal will have been replaced by minerals. It will have become a fossil.

AN IDEAL SHAPE

The best shape for an underwater hunter is a streamlined body with a strong flattened tail and paddle limbs. Many of the Permian, Triassic, Jurassic, and Cretaceous swimming reptiles were built like this as were the tertiary whales. Some had strange adaptations like long necks that probably enabled them to reach prey hiding in rocks.

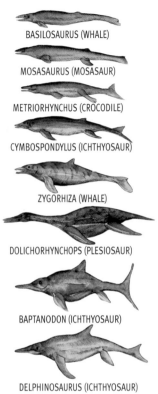

BASILOSAURUS (WHALE)

MOSASAURUS (MOSASAUR)

METRIORHYNCHUS (CROCODILE)

CYMBOSPONDYLUS (ICHTHYOSAUR)

ZYGORHIZA (WHALE)

DOLICHORHYNCHOPS (PLESIOSAUR)

BAPTANODON (ICHTHYOSAUR)

DELPHINOSAURUS (ICHTHYOSAUR)

BIG IS BEAUTIFUL

The biggest turtle known, *Archelon*, cruised the inland sea that covered much of North America in late Cretaceous times. At almost four metres (13 ft) long it was bigger than a rowing boat. Its shell was reduced to a system of bony struts covered by tough skin; much like the biggest of the modern turtles, the leatherback. It probably fed on soft things like jellyfish, as just like the modern leatherback, its jaws were not very strong.

| TRIASSIC 248-206 MYA | EARLY/MID JURASSIC 206-159 MYA | LATE JURASSIC 159-144 MYA | EARLY CRETACEOUS 144-97 MYA | LATE CRETACEOUS 97-65 MYA |

PLACODONTS
THE SHELL SEEKERS

Water-living animals may have evolved from land-living animals for a variety of reasons. Most persuasive of these is the idea that when a good food supply exists, nature will develop something to exploit it. Shellfish represent one such food supply. The earliest reptiles that seemed to be well adapted to feeding on shellfish were the placodonts. Although they still needed to come to the surface to breathe, they rooted on the bed of the Tethys Ocean that spread across southern Europe in Triassic times.

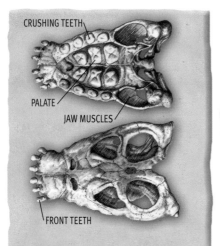

CRUSHING TEETH

PALATE

JAW MUSCLES

FRONT TEETH

POWERFUL BITE

From below, the protruding front teeth of *Placodus* are obvious. These prominent teeth were used for plucking shells from the rocks and the seafloor. Further back, the jaws have strong crushing teeth, and even the palate is paved with broad, flat teeth, all ideal for smashing the shells of shellfish. Holes in the side of the skull show where very powerful jaw muscles were attached. *Placodus* would have eaten brachiopods as well as bivalves similar to those that survive today.

PLACODUS

The most typical of the placodonts was *Placodus* itself. In appearance it looked somewhat like an enormous newt, about 7 feet (2 m) long, with a chunky body, a paddle-shaped tail, webbed feet, and a short head.

BUILT FOR BUOYANCY

A glimpse of the skeleton of *Placodus* reveals one of its main adaptations to an underwater way of life—"pachystosis." This means that its bones were broad and heavy, perfect for feeding on the bottom of the ocean. Animals that have pachystosis also have big lungs to help regulate buoyancy. To accommodate its huge lungs, *Placodus* developed a broad rib cage. A modern animal with these adaptations is the sea otter. Its weight and large lung capacity enable it to walk along the seabed with ease, hunting shellfish. *Placodus* would have done the same.

TRIASSIC 248-206 MYA	EARLY/MID JURASSIC 206-159 MYA	LATE JURASSIC 159-144 MYA	EARLY CRETACEOUS 144-97 MYA	LATE CRETACEOUS 97-65 MYA

A SHELLED FAMILY

Because they were slow-moving animals, the placodonts must have been vulnerable to the meat eaters of the time. Many developed shells on their backs as protection. In some types, the shells were extensive and looked much like those of turtles, but the two groups of animals were not related. The similar shells developed independently among animals with the same lifestyle in the same environment—a process known as "convergent evolution."

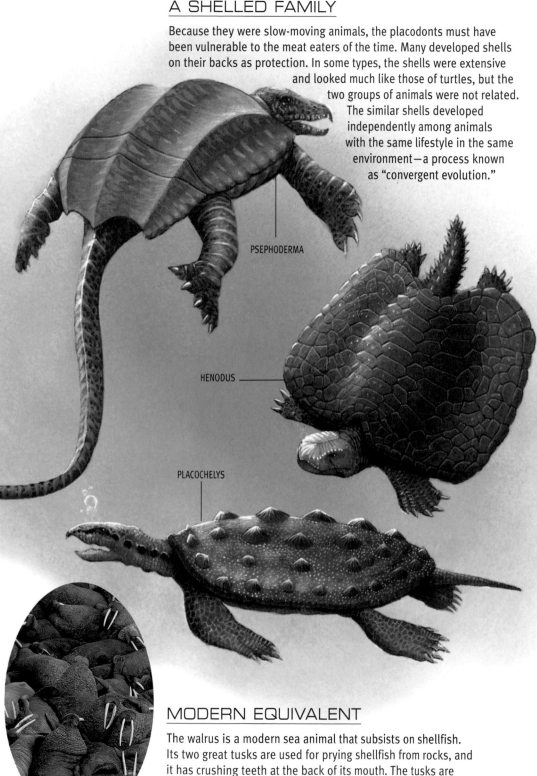

PSEPHODERMA

HENODUS

PLACOCHELYS

MODERN EQUIVALENT

The walrus is a modern sea animal that subsists on shellfish. Its two great tusks are used for prying shellfish from rocks, and it has crushing teeth at the back of its mouth. The tusks are also used as ice picks and for mating displays. We do not know if the protruding teeth of the placodonts had similar functions.

BETWEEN THE LAND & THE SEA

The nothosaurs preceded the plesiosaurs, rulers of the Late Jurassic and Cretaceous seas. Like the placodonts, they are known mostly from sediments laid down in the Tethys Ocean, an ancient ocean that lay between Africa and Europe. Their necks, bodies, and tails were long, and they had webbed feet (although they could walk on land). Their hind limbs were much larger than their front limbs and were used mostly for swimming. They had many small, pointed teeth in long, narrow jaws for catching fish. Nothosaurs seem to represent a stage between land-living animals and fish-eating, seagoing animals like the plesiosaurs.

NOTHOSAURUS

LET'S GO FISHING

The long jaws and sharp teeth of *Nothosaurus* were ideal for catching fish. The long neck would have been able to reach fast-swimming fish quickly, and the little teeth would have held the slippery prey firmly. These teeth can be seen in such modern fish-eating animals as crocodiles.

NOTHOSAUR FOSSIL

Nothosaur fossils have been found in the Alps and in China. Although these animals had legs and toes, their limb bones were not strongly joined to one another and the hips and shoulders were quite weak. This weakened state shows that they were not well adapted to moving on land and were better at swimming than at walking.

TRIASSIC 248-206 MYA	EARLY/MID JURASSIC 206-159 MYA	LATE JURASSIC 159-144 MYA	EARLY CRETACEOUS 144-97 MYA	LATE CRETACEOUS 97-65 MYA

DUCKBILLED PLATYPUS

The duckbilled platypus is a modern animal with many primitive traits, such as webbed feet that push the water back, driving the animal forward. Later marine animals had limbs that evolved into flippers. These flippers were built like wings, allowing the animal to travel through the water using a motion that resembled flying. Nothosaurs seem to represent a stage between the primitive platypus and more advanced sea creatures. Some nothosaurs had webbed feet, while others had paddles.

LARIOSAURUS

CERESIOSAURUS

A VARIETY OF NOTHOSAURS

Although nothosaurs conformed to a particular shape, they displayed much variation within their group. *Nothosaurus* (from which the group gets its name) was 10 feet (3 m) long and had a very long head with jaws full of little teeth. *Lariosaurus*, at 2 feet (60 cm) one of the smallest nothosaurs, was very primitive and looked very much like a land-living animal that happened to be swimming in the sea. Big *Ceresiosaurus*, on the other hand, had feet that were almost like paddles and a small head on a long neck.

THE GIANTS OF THE SEA

The plesiosaurs were perhaps the most varied group of swimming reptiles during the time of the dinosaurs. They were ocean-going fish eaters, ranging in size from the length of a small seal to that of a medium-sized whale. They had broad bodies, short tails, and two pairs of winglike paddles with which they "flew" through ocean waters. One group had short necks and long heads; the other had long necks and very small heads *(see pages 20–23)*. The short-necked types are called pliosaurs, and the long-necked types are elasmosaurs.

UNDERWATER ATTACK

From this evidence, we can build up a picture of a Late Jurassic marine incident. A long-necked elasmosaur feeds near the surface. A pliosaur cruises at some depth below, hunting fish and squid. By tasting the water, it knows the elasmosaur is nearby. Vomiting out a few stomach stones, it adjusts its buoyancy to allow it to rise. Then, when its prey is in view, the pliosaur "flies" toward the elasmosaur with strong thrusts of its flippers, closing in on a paddle and ripping it apart with its teeth.

IN FOR THE KILL

Broad flanges at the back of the skull of a pliosaur must have held massive neck muscles, suggesting that pliosaurs grabbed their larger prey and pulled it to bits with a twisting action. Crocodiles in deep water dismember their food in exactly this way today.

BIG MOUTH

The most amazing feature of a pliosaur skeleton is its huge skull. The long jaws were equipped with many sharp teeth that were ideal for catching big fish and squid and also for seizing larger prey. The nostrils are surprisingly small and would not have been used for breathing. Instead, they would have been used for tasting the water and for judging the speed at which the animal was swimming. A pliosaur probably breathed through its mouth when it came to the surface.

PLIOSAUR TOOTH MARKS

The limb bones of an elasmosaur found in Late Jurassic marine rocks in Dorset, England, have given scientists a dramatic clue to the feeding habits of the pliosaurs. Tooth marks punched deep into the bones match the set of teeth of a big pliosaur. Until this discovery, scientists thought that pliosaurs ate only fish and squid.

STOMACH STONES

Most good fossilized skeletons of pliosaurs contain collections of gastroliths (stomach stones). Sea-living animals swallow stones to help adjust their ballast (weight). For animals that swim fast to catch their prey, this method is a more versatile system than building up the weight of the skeleton through pachystosis, a method adopted by the placodonts (*see pages 12–13*).

| TRIASSIC 248-206 MYA | EARLY/MID JURASSIC 206-159 MYA | LATE JURASSIC 159-144 MYA | EARLY CRETACEOUS 144-97 MYA | LATE CRETACEOUS 97-65 MYA |

A RANGE OF PLIOSAURS

We used to think that pliosaurs were the biggest sea reptiles of all time. This was until we found the remains of beasts that were even bigger *(see page 27)*. Nevertheless, the biggest pliosaurs were very big animals. Many smaller pliosaurs also cruised the seas. Their different sizes and head shapes reflected their different lifestyles and the different foods they were eating. Some must have lived like penguins, darting and snatching at the weaving and dispersing schools of fish, but the biggest must have been the dolphins and toothed whales of their time. Often, all we know of a particular pliosaur is the skull. Using the skull as a guide and building models based on an agreed-upon plan, scientists have assumed that we can know what the rest of the body was like. Who knows for sure if they are right?

LIOPLEURODON VERTEBRA

This is a vertebra from *Liopleurodon*, which existed in northern European waters at the end of the Jurassic Period. Pliosaurs were a wide-ranging group, with very similar animals existing in Europe at one time and on the other side of the world in Australia 80 million years later. It was probably *Liopleurodon* that attacked the elasmosaur in the incident described on page 16.

MONSTER OF THE DEEP

We used to think that the skull of the pliosaur *Kronosaurus* represented less than a quarter of the length of the whole animal, giving *Kronosaurus* a total length of 40–46 feet (12–14 m) —greater than the contemporary *Tyrannosaurus* on land. More recent studies suggest that the skull was about a third of the total length, making it 26 feet (8 m) long. That's still quite a monster!

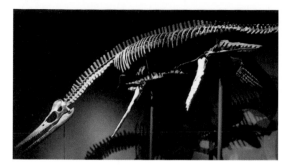

SUPER-PENGUINS

Dolichorhynchops was a much smaller pliosaur, about 10 feet (3 m) long. It lived in the seas that covered Late Cretaceous Manitoba in Canada. Judging the animal by its build and its teeth, scientists feel that it swam easily among schools of fish that frequented the waters, snapping them up in its long, narrow jaws. It swam like modern penguins, using paddles to get around.

A HALFWAY STAGE

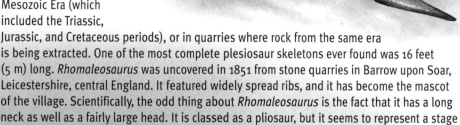

Fossilized bones of sea animals are much more common than those of land animals. They are often found on beaches, where the sea is eroding cliffs made of rock from the Mesozoic Era (which included the Triassic, Jurassic, and Cretaceous periods), or in quarries where rock from the same era is being extracted. One of the most complete plesiosaur skeletons ever found was 16 feet (5 m) long. *Rhomaleosaurus* was uncovered in 1851 from stone quarries in Barrow upon Soar, Leicestershire, central England. It featured widely spread ribs, and it has become the mascot of the village. Scientifically, the odd thing about *Rhomaleosaurus* is the fact that it has a long neck as well as a fairly large head. It is classed as a pliosaur, but it seems to represent a stage between the short-necked pliosaurs and the long-necked elasmosaurs.

TRIASSIC	EARLY/MID JURASSIC	LATE JURASSIC	EARLY CRETACEOUS	LATE CRETACEOUS
248-206 MYA	206-159 MYA	159-144 MYA	144-97 MYA	97-65 MYA

ELASMOSAURS
THE LONG NECKS

One early researcher described the long-necked plesiosaurs as "snakes threaded through turtles." A plesiosaur's broad body and winglike flippers are like an oceangoing turtle, but its long neck and small head full of vicious pointed teeth are very different from the placid shelled reptile that we know today. Elasmosaurs were the sea serpents of their time. They existed alongside pliosaurs in the oceans of the Jurassic and Cretaceous periods.

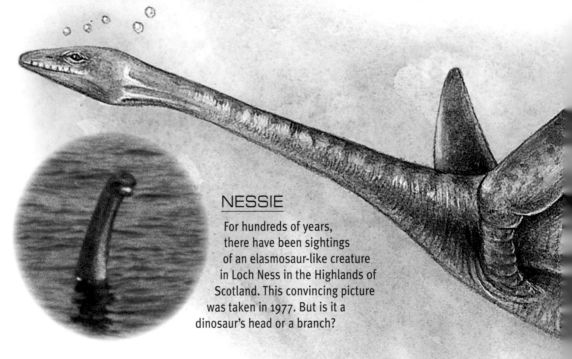

NESSIE

For hundreds of years, there have been sightings of an elasmosaur-like creature in Loch Ness in the Highlands of Scotland. This convincing picture was taken in 1977. But is it a dinosaur's head or a branch?

ARTISTIC IMPRESSIONS

Because of numerous fossils, the remains of plesiosaurs had been known to fossil collectors for a long time before dinosaurs were discovered. This 19th-century engraving of a prehistoric coastal scene shows a giant ichthyosaur being attacked by two long-necked plesiosaurs. Although far from perfect, depictions of sea creatures were much more accurate than those of land-living dinosaurs from the same period.

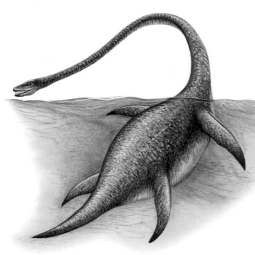

FLEXIBILITY

The great length of the elasmosaur neck with its huge number of vertebrae has led some to suggest that it would have been as flexible as a snake. But looking at the way the vertebrae are articulated, this is not completely true. From side to side there was a good degree of movement, but the neck was restricted in the up-and-down plane. Although an elasmosaur could reach downward with ease, it could not hold its head up like a swan on the surface.

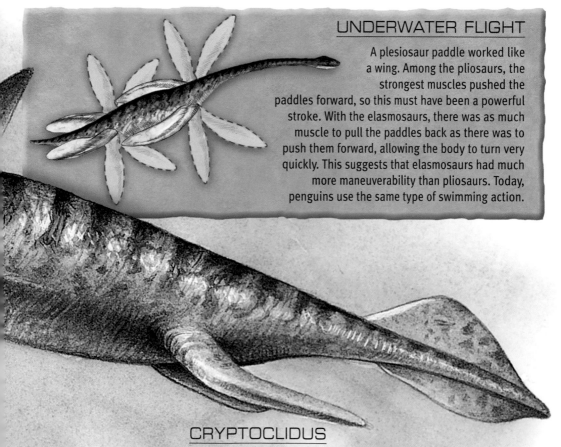

UNDERWATER FLIGHT

A plesiosaur paddle worked like a wing. Among the pliosaurs, the strongest muscles pushed the paddles forward, so this must have been a powerful stroke. With the elasmosaurs, there was as much muscle to pull the paddles back as there was to push them forward, allowing the body to turn very quickly. This suggests that elasmosaurs had much more maneuverability than pliosaurs. Today, penguins use the same type of swimming action.

CRYPTOCLIDUS

Cryptoclidus was a common elasmosaur found in late Jurassic rocks of Europe. Its mounted skeleton can be seen in several museums. It is typical of the entire elasmosaur group, with its broad body with ribs above and below, long neck, mouth full of sharp outward-pointing teeth, and paddles made up of packed bone.

TRIASSIC 248-206 MYA	EARLY/MID JURASSIC 206-159 MYA	LATE JURASSIC 159-144 MYA	EARLY CRETACEOUS 144-97 MYA	LATE CRETACEOUS 97-65 MYA

ELASMOSAUR LIFESTYLE

Elasmosaurs came in all sizes. As time went by, the group displayed a tendency to develop longer and longer necks. They may have hunted by ambush. The big body was probably used to disturb schools of fish, while the little head at the end of the long neck darted quickly into the group and speared individual fish on the long teeth. Moving the paddles in different directions would have turned the body very quickly in any direction. Their agility meant that elasmosaurs probably hunted on the surface, as opposed to the pliosaurs, which were built for sustained cruising at great depths.

ELASMOSAURUS

We take the name of the elasmosaur group from Late Cretaceous *Elasmosaurus*. This creature had the longest neck, in proportion to the body, of any animal known. It had 71 vertebrae, in contrast to the 28 or so of the earlier elasmosaurs. The neck took up more than half the length of the entire animal.

TEETH PUZZLE

In most elasmosaurs, the sharp pointed teeth most likely evolved for catching fish. But in some types, such as *Hydrotherosaurus*, the teeth seem to be the wrong shape. Although they are long and pointed, they jut outward, which would have made holding slippery prey difficult. It is possible that these elasmosaurs used this tooth arrangement as a kind of a trap to catch very small fish or invertebrates. On the other hand, they could have used the teeth as a rake for sifting mud and sand on the seabed.

TRIASSIC 248-206 MYA	EARLY/MID JURASSIC 206-159 MYA	LATE JURASSIC 159-144 MYA	EARLY CRETACEOUS 144-97 MYA	LATE CRETACEOUS 97-65 MYA

GIVING BIRTH

Most reptiles lay eggs. Reptile eggs have hard shells through which the developing embryo can breathe. Unfortunately, reptiles thus cannot lay their eggs at sea, because the young would drown. It is possible that elasmosaurs laid eggs the way modern turtles do. This would mean that they came ashore at certain times of the year and scooped out a hole in the beach with their flippers. This process is a great effort for a modern turtle. Just imagine the effort for a 39-foot (12-m) plesiosaur!

SURVIVING TODAY?

Now and then we hear stories of people sighting sea serpents that have a distinct similarity to plesiosaurs. Several photographs exist of rotting carcasses with a plesiosaur look to them. The carcasses usually turn out to be those of basking sharks. Although a basking shark looks nothing like a plesiosaur in life, its dead body deteriorates in a particular pattern. The dorsal fin and the tail fin fall off, losing the shark's distinctive profile. Then the massive jaws drop away. This leaves a tiny brain case at the end of a long string of vertebrae. Instant plesiosaur!

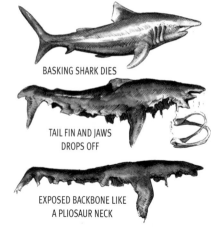

BASKING SHARK DIES

TAIL FIN AND JAWS DROPS OFF

EXPOSED BACKBONE LIKE A PLIOSAUR NECK

CRETACEOUS ELASMOSAUR   CRETACEOUS PLIOSAUR

JURASSIC PLIOSAUR

THE "POLYPHYLETIC" THEORY

It is possible that elasmosaurs were "polyphyletic," which means they did not evolve from one ancestor. The Jurassic elasmosaurs evolved from the same ancestors as the nothosaurs of the Triassic Period. However, the arrangement of the skull bones of the Cretaceous elasmosaurs has led some scientists to suggest that these later ones actually evolved from the short-necked pliosaurs of the Jurassic Period. The long neck developed independently in response to environmental pressures; there was food to be had for long-necked animals, so long-necked animals evolved. Most scientists, however, believe that all the elasmosaurs evolved from the same ancestors—that is, they were "monophyletic."

ICHTHYOSAURS
THE FISH LIZARDS

Without doubt, the most well-adapted marine reptiles of the Mesozoic were the ichthyosaurs. If you saw one swimming, you might mistake it for a dolphin or even a shark. It is all there—the streamlined body, the triangular fin on the back, the big swimming fin on the tail, and the paired swimming organs at the side. Like dolphins, ichthyosaurs were descended from land-living animals and needed to come to the surface to breathe. Although some ichthyosaurs continued into the Late Cretaceous, mosasaurs became the dominant marine reptile during that time *(see pages 30–31)*.

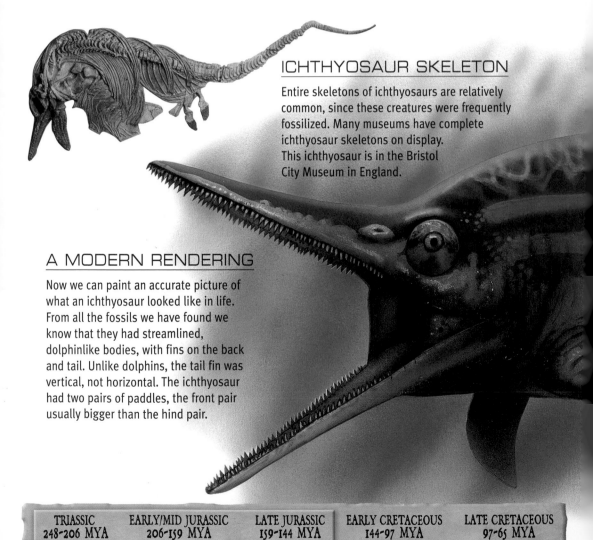

ICHTHYOSAUR SKELETON

Entire skeletons of ichthyosaurs are relatively common, since these creatures were frequently fossilized. Many museums have complete ichthyosaur skeletons on display. This ichthyosaur is in the Bristol City Museum in England.

A MODERN RENDERING

Now we can paint an accurate picture of what an ichthyosaur looked like in life. From all the fossils we have found we know that they had streamlined, dolphinlike bodies, with fins on the back and tail. Unlike dolphins, the tail fin was vertical, not horizontal. The ichthyosaur had two pairs of paddles, the front pair usually bigger than the hind pair.

TRIASSIC 248-206 MYA	EARLY/MID JURASSIC 206-159 MYA	LATE JURASSIC 159-144 MYA	EARLY CRETACEOUS 144-97 MYA	LATE CRETACEOUS 97-65 MYA

AN ICHTHYOSAUR PIONEER

As with the plesiosaurs, the ichthyosaurs were known before the dinosaurs. Early naturalists, who discovered them in eroding cliffs along the Dorset coast in southern England, took them for the remains of ancient crocodiles. Indeed, their long jaws and sharp teeth are very reminiscent of crocodiles. Mary Anning (1799–1847), a professional fossil collector and dealer from Lyme Regis in Dorset, is credited with finding the first complete fossil ichthyosaur when she was 12 years old. This is a myth, but her collecting and her dealings with the scientists of the day were crucial in furthering our knowledge of these creatures.

A CLEAR IMAGE

Thinly layered, Late-Jurassic rocks at Holzmaden in Germany are so fine that they contain the impressions of the softest organisms that lived and died there. The bottom of the sea (where the rocks formed) was so stagnant that nothing lived—not even the bacteria that normally break down once-living matter. Among the spectacular fossils found there are the ichthyosaurs, with impressions of their soft anatomy still preserved. Flesh and skin still exist as a fine film of the original carbon. With this find, scientists were able to determine for the first time that ichthyosaurs had a dorsal fin and a big, fishlike fin on the tail.

A RANGE OF ICHTHYOSAURS

Before the standard dolphin shape of the ichthyosaur evolved, this creature came in many different shapes and sizes, particularly among the earlier ichthyosaurs in the Triassic seas. These different types had different lifestyles and swimming techniques. Some were long and narrow like eels, without a significant tail fin. They probably swam with a flying motion, like the plesiosaurs and penguins, and steered with their long tails. Some were the size of whales, with increased bone mass to make them heavier and able to swim in deep water for long periods. This range of Triassic forms soon settled to the classic dolphin shape of the Jurassic ichthyosaur.

CYMBOSPONDYLUS

MIXOSAURUS

OPHTHALMOSAURUS

MEET THE FAMILY

Probably the most primitive-looking ichthyosaur was *Cymbospondylus,* found in the Middle Triassic rocks of Nevada. Measuring 33 feet (10 m), it was a big animal, but its body was long and eel-like. *Mixosaurus,* found in Middle Triassic rocks from around the world, was still long and slim, but it showed the beginnings of the typical ichthyosaur tail. The 49-foot (15-m) monster *Shonisaurus,* from the late Triassic rocks of Nevada, was the biggest ichthyosaur known before the discovery of the Canadian giant *(see page 27). Opthalmosaurus* was probably the most fishlike and had no teeth in its jaws. It may have fed on soft-bodied animals like squid. *Eurhinosaurus* had a swordfish-like beak on its upper jaw. It possibly used this beak for stunning fish prey.

TRIASSIC	EARLY/MID JURASSIC	LATE JURASSIC	EARLY CRETACEOUS	LATE CRETACEOUS
248-206 MYA	206-159 MYA	159-144 MYA	144-97 MYA	97-65 MYA

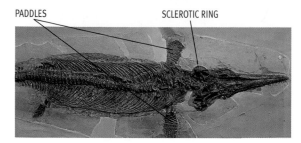

PADDLES   SCLEROTIC RING

ICHTHYOSAUR ANATOMY

Most ichthyosaurs had big eyes. A ring of bone inside each eye (the sclerotic ring) supported it against water pressure. Like plesiosaurs, they showed hyperphalangy (an increase in the number of joints in the finger), but they also showed hyperdactyly (an increase in the number of fingers). This improved the rigidity of the paddles, which were solid bone.

TRIASSIC GIANT

A truly enormous Triassic ichthyosaur was discovered in British Columbia, Canada, in 1998. At 75 feet (23 m), it was longer than a sperm whale and approached the length of most blue whales. The skeleton is 30 percent longer than any other marine reptile so far discovered, and its head is 19 feet (5.8 m) long. It has been identified as a species of Shonisaurus.

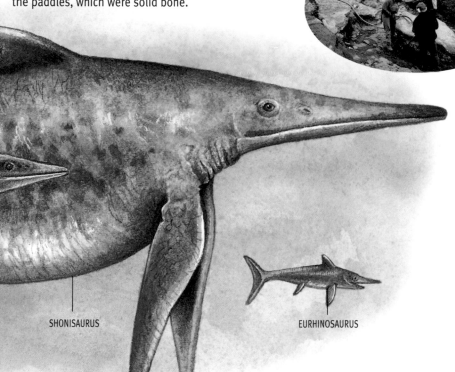

SHONISAURUS   EURHINOSAURUS

SWIMMING

An ichthyosaur's swimming motion (at least that of the dolphin-shaped ichthyosaurs) depended on the complex interaction of thrust and the center of balance. The tail gave a forward and upward thrust directed through the center of balance, and the paddles adjusted the trim. Curving itself in a vertical plane, the ichthyosaur could dive and surface. The easiest way to turn would be to execute this movement and use its paddles to roll itself onto its side.

TAIL   PADDLES

ICHTHYOSAURS
DISPELLING A MYTH

The fact that reptiles lay eggs on land is what distinguishes them from their ancestors, the amphibians. Occasionally, however, reptiles that live in harsh environments in which exposed eggs would be vulnerable tend to give birth to live young. Most of the modern reptiles that live in northern Europe, such as the common lizard, the slow worm, and the adder, bear live young. The ichthyosaurs also did this.

FISH FOOD

Belemnites were squidlike animals that swarmed in the warm shallow seas of the Jurassic Period. Like squid, they had tentacles that were armed with tiny hooks, but unlike squid, their bodies were stiffened with bullet-shaped internal shells. These shells are commonly found as fossils in Jurassic rocks. We know that many ichthyosaurs ate belemnites, because we have found masses of their indigestible hooks in the stomach areas of ichthyosaur fossils.

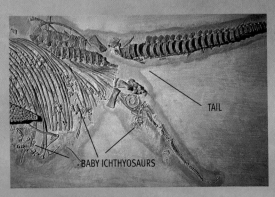

TAIL

BABY ICHTHYOSAURS

LITTLE ONES

This ichthyosaur from Holzmaden in Germany has been preserved with the broken-up skeletons of three unborn young still intact. A fourth may just have been born. Its skeleton can be seen below the tail of the parent. The mother must have died while giving birth underwater.

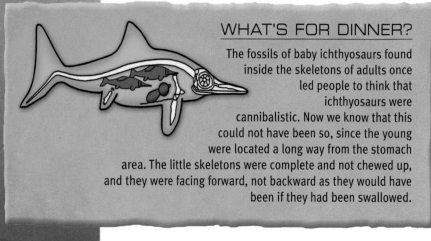

HOLZMADEN

In Late Jurassic times, a shallow sea with scattered islands covered most of northern Europe. To the north was low-lying land, and to the south, beyond a series of massive reefs formed by corals and sponges, lay the open ocean. The region of Holzmaden may have been a seasonal gathering place where ichthyosaurs came to give birth. We can tell much about the ichthyosaurs' anatomy and lifestyle from fossils found in the region. A large number of ichthyosaur remains shows baby ichthyosaurs emerging from the adult. These remains tell us that ichthyosaur birth was a very traumatic event that sometimes proved fatal for the mother.

TRIASSIC	EARLY/MID JURASSIC	LATE JURASSIC	EARLY CRETACEOUS	LATE CRETACEOUS
248-206 MYA	206-159 MYA	159-144 MYA	144-97 MYA	97-65 MYA

MOSASAURS

In 1770, workmen in a chalk quarry near Maastricht in Holland uncovered a long-jawed, toothy skull. The owner of the land sued for possession—a circumstance that is all too common in the field of paleontology, even today. In 1794, the French army invaded Holland and, despite the owner's attempt to hide the skull in a cave, seized it and took it back to Paris. There it was studied by the legendary French anatomist Baron Georges Cuvier. By this time it had been identified as the skull of a huge reptile related to the modern monitor lizards. British geologist William Conybeare gave it the name *Mosasaurus* ("lizard from the Meuse").

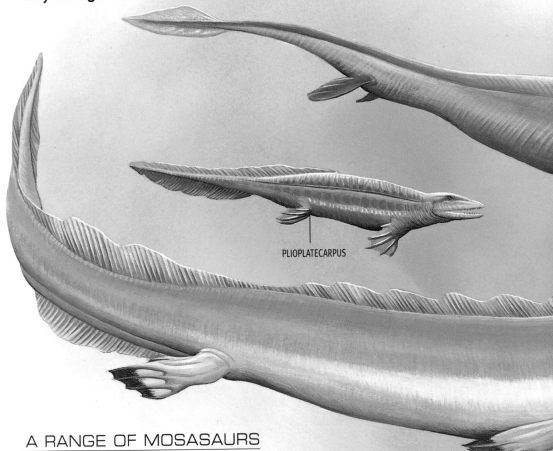

PLIOPLATECARPUS

A RANGE OF MOSASAURS

Mosasaurs are known from Late Cretaceous deposits throughout the world. They were all based on a similar body plan and ranged in size from a few feet to monsters 33 feet (10 m) or more in length. Their heads were all very similar to those of the modern monitor lizard, and their teeth had adapted to snatch at fish or ammonites. An exception was *Globidens*, which had flattened, rounded teeth that were obviously adapted to a shellfish diet.

TRIASSIC 248-206 MYA	EARLY/MID JURASSIC 206-159 MYA	LATE JURASSIC 159-144 MYA	EARLY CRETACEOUS 144-97 MYA	LATE CRETACEOUS 97-65 MYA

DINNER TIME

There is direct evidence that mosasaurs ate the abundant ammonites of the time. The ammonites were relatives of the modern squid and nautilus and displayed coiled shells that are very common as fossils. They lived throughout the Mesozoic in seas all over the world. One ammonite fossil has been found punctured by tooth marks that exactly match those of a small mosasaur. Evidently, the reptile had to bite the ammonite sixteen times before crushing the shell and reaching the animal.

FAMILY MEMBER?

The bones of *Mosasaurus* were very similar to those of the modern monitor lizard. Despite the extinction of individual species, the same lines of animals were continuing to develop into other forms. The concept of evolution that would explain such phenomena had not been developed when *Mosasaurus* was first studied.

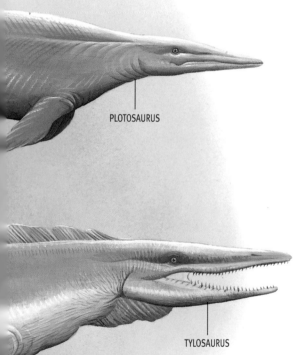

PLOTOSAURUS

TYLOSAURUS

GEORGES CUVIER

Baron Georges Cuvier (1769–1832) was impressed by the jawbones of an unknown giant reptile unearthed from underground quarries near the River Meuse. The French anatomist became convinced that there were once animals living on Earth that were completely unlike modern types and that these ancient animals were periodically wiped out by extinction events.

A SWIMMING LIZARD

The aigialosaurs were ancestors of the mosasaurs. They were a group of swimming lizards that lived in Europe during the Late Jurassic and Early to Middle Cretaceous periods. They grew to 3 feet (1 m) long and had flattened tails but lacked the specialized paddle limbs of their descendants.

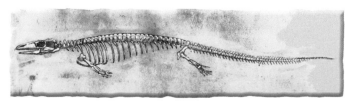

CROCODILES

Crocodiles have remained essentially unaltered since Late Triassic times. Throughout their history, however, crocodiles have adapted to many conditions. Some were long-legged and scampered about on land, while some ran on hind legs like little versions of their relatives, the dinosaurs. More significantly, some developed into sea-living forms showing the same adaptations as other sea-living reptiles—the sinuous bodies, the paddle legs, and the finned tails. These features were particularly important in Jurassic times.

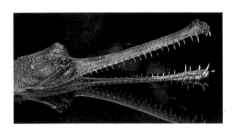

MODERN GHARIAL

In life, *Steneosaurus* must have looked very much like the modern gharial of the Indian rivers—the same long narrow jaws with the many sharp fish-catching teeth, the same long body and tail, and the same short legs. The gharial is a river animal, however, while *Steneosaurus* hunted in the sea.

A SELECTION OF SEA CROCS

Teleosaurus was a gharial-like sea crocodile. It was even longer and slimmer in build than *Steneosaurus*. *Metriorhynchus* was 10 feet (3 m) long and shows much more extreme adaptations to a seagoing way of life. It lacked the armored scales that we see on more conventional crocodiles. Its legs were converted into paddles that would have been almost useless on land. At the end of its tail the vertebral column was turned downward, showing that it had a swimming fin like an ichthyosaur. This was a true sea crocodile. *Geosaurus* had the same adaptations as *Metriorhynchus* but appeared somewhat later and, at 7 feet (2 m) long, was considerably smaller. It was much slimmer, and the jaws were even narrower.

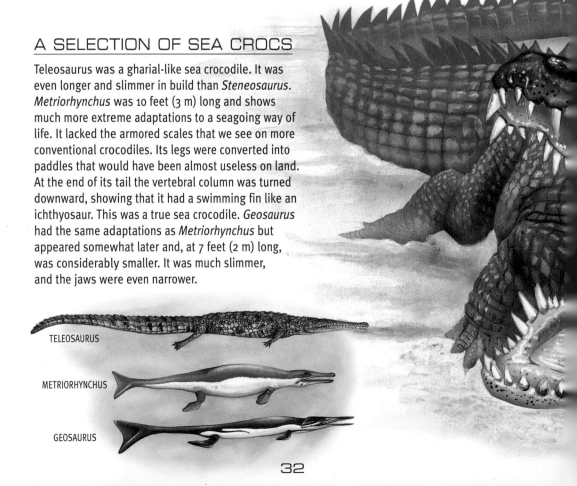

TELEOSAURUS

METRIORHYNCHUS

GEOSAURUS

CHAMPSOSAUR

PHYTOSAUR

CROCODILE

A GOOD SHAPE

Many semi-aquatic, meat-eating reptiles have crocodile shapes. The phytosaurs from the Late Triassic could be mistaken for crocodiles except for their nostrils, which were close to the eyes instead of at the tip of the snout. The champsosaurs from the Late Cretaceous of North America were also very crocodile-like, having the same lifestyle in the same habitat. None of these animals was closely related to another. This pattern is an example of "parallel evolution."

STENEOSAURUS

The fine shales that preserved the ichthyosaurs in the Holzmaden quarries were also very successful in preserving the marine crocodile *Steneosaurus*. We can see that it was very much like a modern crocodile. Although its legs and feet show it to have been an animal that spent much of its time on land, the occurrence of its fossils at Holzmaden and in marine deposits in England show that it was also a seagoing beast. The position of its eyes (on the top of its head) reminds us of the crocodile and alligator of today.

LIKE TODAY?

Looking at *Deinosuchus* from a distance, you would think it was a modern crocodile. Indeed, it belonged to the same family as modern crocodiles, although it lived in the Late Cretaceous. But then you notice its size—49 feet (15 m) long! This monster ate dinosaurs!

TRIASSIC 248-206 MYA	EARLY/MID JURASSIC 206-159 MYA	LATE JURASSIC 159-144 MYA	EARLY CRETACEOUS 144-97 MYA	LATE CRETACEOUS 97-65 MYA

WHAT CAME NEXT?

The great extinction event at the end of the Cretaceous period that wiped out the dinosaurs and other big land-living animals had an even greater effect on the sea. A vast number of the invertebrates (including the ammonites and the belemnites) disappeared, and with them went the big reptiles. The placodonts and the ichthyosaurs had already died out, but suddenly the elasmosaurs, the pliosaurs and the mosasaurs disappeared too, as did the pterosaurs that winged their way overhead. This left the oceans wide open to be repopulated by something else—the mammals.

A TEMPORARY MEASURE

As mammals established their supremacy on our planet, a peculiar group of sea mammals cropped up. Called the desmostylians, they were as big as horses. They had strange, stumpy, inward-turned feet that they probably used for walking across the seabed like a hippopotamus. Their teeth consisted of a bunch of forward-pointing tusks forming a structure that resembles a shovel. These were probably used for grazing seaweed or even plucking shellfish, and crushing teeth at the back of the jaws would have been suitable for either. The desmostylians were a short-lived group and died out without leaving any descendants. Other than noticing their resemblence to the walrus, we cannot really compare them with anything that is alive today.

INSTEAD OF THE PLESIOSAURS

Sea lions today remind us of plesiosaurs as they pursue fish using the flying movements of their flippers. Even more striking is the resemblance between the ancient ichthyosaurs and dolphins, especially in the similarity of their shapes.

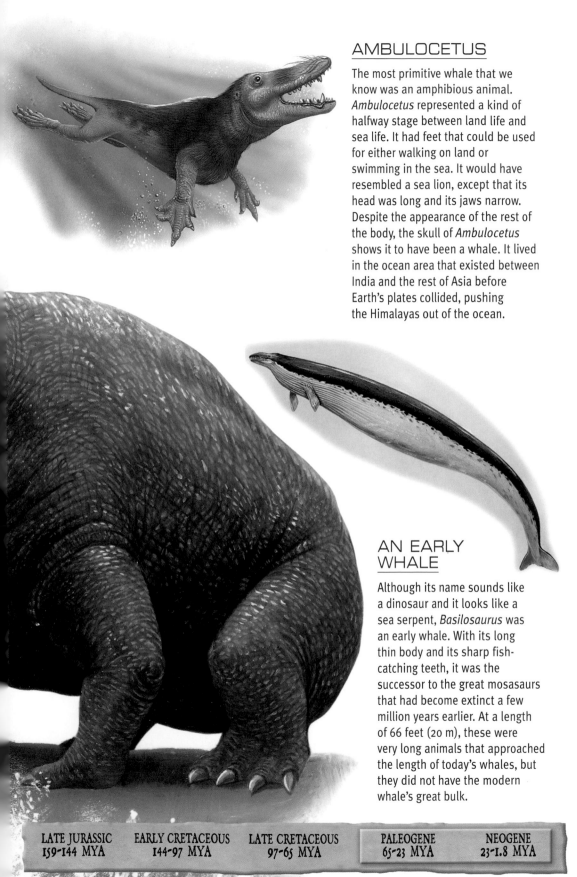

AMBULOCETUS

The most primitive whale that we know was an amphibious animal. *Ambulocetus* represented a kind of halfway stage between land life and sea life. It had feet that could be used for either walking on land or swimming in the sea. It would have resembled a sea lion, except that its head was long and its jaws narrow. Despite the appearance of the rest of the body, the skull of *Ambulocetus* shows it to have been a whale. It lived in the ocean area that existed between India and the rest of Asia before Earth's plates collided, pushing the Himalayas out of the ocean.

AN EARLY WHALE

Although its name sounds like a dinosaur and it looks like a sea serpent, *Basilosaurus* was an early whale. With its long thin body and its sharp fish-catching teeth, it was the successor to the great mosasaurs that had become extinct a few million years earlier. At a length of 66 feet (20 m), these were very long animals that approached the length of today's whales, but they did not have the modern whale's great bulk.

| LATE JURASSIC 159-144 MYA | EARLY CRETACEOUS 144-97 MYA | LATE CRETACEOUS 97-65 MYA | PALEOGENE 65-23 MYA | NEOGENE 23-1.8 MYA |

DID YOU KNOW?

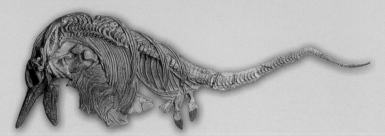

The state fossil of Nevada is the giant ichthyosaur *Shonisaurus*.

It was not just the reptiles that went back to the water in the age of the dinosaurs. A Jurassic mammal did so too. *Castorocauda*, from the middle Jurassic of Mongolia took up an otter-like existence.

The first specimen of *Elasmosaurus* to have been mounted in a museum was in 1868. Unfortunately the paleontologists were confused by the long neck and, thinking that it was the tail, the skull was then mounted on the wrong end! The palaeontologist who was responsible was mocked by his great scientific rival and this led to one of the most bitter and long-lasting feuds in paleontological history.

Plesiosaurs are often misinterpreted in this way. Just recently it was found that the fossil of the hindquarters and part of the tail of an elasmosaur found in Greenland in the 1930s was actually the forequarters and part of the neck. Other individual bones have been misinterpreted as well, with hip bones turning out to be shoulder bones and such like. Perhaps the biggest blunder of this kind was the discovery of a plated stegosaur dinosaur, called *Dravidosaurus*, in India—from a time and a place where it is unlikely that there ever were stegosaurs. The fossilized plates turned out to be plesiosaur limb bones.

We really do not know the purpose of the armor of some of the placodonts (*see pages 12–13*). There were no big marine predators at the time that would have been capable of attacking them.

Sea crocodile teeth are far more common in Jurassic sea sediments than their bones. That is because the teeth were shed throughout their lives, and were covered in hard enamel that stopped them from decaying before they were fossilized.

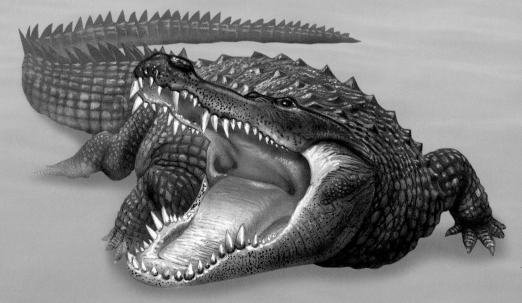

Ichthyosaurs had very flattened eyeballs. There was a ring of little bones in the eye—the sclerotic ring—that helped to keep the eyeball in shape. The large eyes were vulnerable to being pushed out of shape by the pressure of the water while diving into deep water after their prey.

There was once a theory that the ichthyosaurs were so bizarre and specialized that they could not have evolved from land-living reptiles but evolved directly from aquatic amphibians without going through a terrestrial phase. This is no longer believed, since advanced computer imagery has shown that the giant primitive forms of the Triassic were actually quite closely related to lizard-like animals that were living on land at the time.

When the skeleton of *Shonisaurus* (*see page 26*) was found in British Columbia in 1998, it was so big that its size could only be appreciated through aerial photography.

As well as the obviously marine reptiles, there were many shoreline types as well that may or may not have spent time in the water. One spectacular one is *Tanystropheus* from the middle Triassic of southern Europe, particularly Italy. It was up to 20 feet (6 m) long, and of this 10 feet (3 m) was neck. When the elongated neck bones were first found they were thought to have been the arm bones of a pterosaur. The jaws in its little head were very much like a fish-hunter's jaws, and so it has been suggested that *Tanystropheus* lived by rock pools ducking in to catch fish.

Just as amazing as all these vertebrate animals, the Mesozoic oceans were full of invertebrates as well. Perhaps the most important were the ammonites. These were relatives of the squid and octopus, and they lived in coiled shells. Every species was different. Some had tightly coiled shells while others had loosely coiled shells, some were decorated with curved ribs while others were decorated by tubercles, some were flat and disc-like while others were broad and squat. These shapes evolved rapidly and became extinct just as quickly. So now, after two centuries of study, scientists can look at the rocks in which their fossils are found and are able to date these rocks by the species of ammonite that they find there. That is why we can put such accurate dates on all the animals that we find fossilized in these rocks. Fossils used in this way are called index fossils.

SUMMARY TIMELINE

CRYPTOCLIDUS

Hovasaurus
Mesosaurus

**PENNSYLVANIAN/
PERMIAN BOUNDARY**

*Cryptoclidus
Rhomaleosaurus
Eurhinosaurus
Temnodontosaurus*

**TRIASSIC/JURASSIC
BOUNDARY**

*Baptanodon
Liopleurodon
Steneosaurus*

**MIDDLE/UPPER
JURASSIC
BOUNDARY**

299   200   161

300   251   175

**PERMIAN/
TRIASSIC
BOUNDARY**

**LOWER/
MIDDLE
JURASSIC
BOUNDARY**

Shonissaurus   Dinocephalosaurus
Proganochelys   Henodus
Odontochelys   Placochelys
Psephoderma   Placodus
Delphinosaurus   Nothosaurus
Mixosaurus   Lariosaurus
Cymbospondylus   Ceresiosaurus
Tanystropheus   Phytosaur

*Castorcauda
Opthalmosaurus
Teleosaurus
Geosaurus
Metriorhynchus
Leedsichthys*

Spinoaequalis

**MISSISSIPPIAN/PENNSYLVANIAN
BOUNDARY**

318

370   300

Champsosaur
Elasmosaurus
Plotosaurus
Tylosaurus
Plioplatecarpus
Styxosaurus
Deinosuchus
Hydrotherosaurus
Archelon
Mosasaurus
Dolichorhynchops

**LOWER/UPPER
CRETACEOUS
BOUNDARY**

PLIOPLATECARPUS

99

145

**JURASSIC/
CRETACEOUS
BOUNDARY**

*Kronosaurus
Dakosaurus
Hyphalosaurus*

100

65

**UPPER CRETACEOUS/
TERTIARY BOUNDARY**

*Desmostylan
Zygorhyza
Basilosaurus
Ambulocetus*

0

million
years ago

KRONOSAURUS

DESMOSTYLAN

WHERE DID THEY LIVE?

Where did prehistoric sea creatures live? They lived in the sea, of course. And as the sea covers over two thirds of the earth's surface, and despite the movements of the continents, has done since the times that the first fossils were formed, we can expect to find fossils of sea animals all over the world.

This is largely true, as the vast majority of sedimentary rocks that exist are rocks that formed at the bottom of the sea. The other consideration is the fact that the sea holds few barriers to swimming organisms. In the present day blue whales are found from the North Atlantic to the South Pacific, killer whales live in the Bering Straits and around Australia. By the same token ancient sea reptiles lived all over the world. We find fossil mosasaurs in late Cretaceous sedimentary rocks of New Zealand and of Kansas. The same kind of plesiosaur fossils lie in the cliffs of southern England as in Russia and South America.

At the beginning of the age of reptiles, in Triassic times, many sea-living reptiles existed on the shelf seas around the Tethys ocean. Back in those days all the earth's continents were fused together in one great supercontinent that we call Pangaea, leaving all the sea areas as one great superocean that we call Panthalassa. Pangaea was almost divided in two by a vast embayment of the ocean. This separated the southern landmass that consisted of the areas destined to become South America, India, Australia and Antarctica, from the northern landmass that consisted of everything else. The embayment is called the Tethys, and the remains of marine creatures are abundant in the sediments that were laid down along its shorelines. Northern Italy has many good fossil sites dating from this time.

As the Jurassic period drew on, many of the low-lying areas of the continents became flooded as shallow shelf oceans spread everywhere. Central Europe, despite being far from the oceans, was covered in such a shallow sea, and we find the most beautifully fossilized ichthyosaur specimens in Germany, so finely preserved in the quiet waters that even the outlines of their fins are visible at the present day.

In areas of active mountain building we find rocks that have been wrenched up from the ocean depths and carried up into the heights of the great fold mountain belts of the world. So in such places we can find the remains of animals whose bodies settled into the deepest ocean. This is the origin of the big ichthyosaur fossils found in the coast ranges of North America. The continent is pushing westward all the time, scraping up the sediments of the ocean floor, along with their fossils, and lifting them well above sea level.

Across the mid-west of the United States, in Cretaceous times, there spread another shallow ocean. It stretched from north to south, from the Arctic Circle to the Gulf of Mexico, and cut the continent completely in two. Nowhere was this sea deeper than about 600 feet (183 m). We know all about it because of the deposits of shale, formed from mud, followed by the deposits of chalk, formed from the shells of microscopic animals, that spread across Kansas, Nebraska, and Wyoming. This is a famous area for the fossils of the sea reptiles that lived at the end of the age of reptiles, particularly the mosasaurs and the plesiosaurs of the time. Although the specimens found there are very good, they are quite thin in the ground. Plesiosaurs consist of only about one percent of the fossils found there.

In the world of the future the rocks being formed today will contain the fossils of the animals that live here now. A future paleontologist will be hard put to find the fossil skeleton of an elephant or a buffalo, but will be more likely to find fossils of whales and seals — the sea beasts of today.

NEW DISCOVERIES

Remains of the biggest pliosaur found so far were unearthed on the Jurassic Coast of southern England in 2009. The pieces of the jaw suggest that the whole animal would have been about 50 feet (16 m) long.

Another, almost the same size, was found in Svalbard in 2008.

The most primitive turtle known is *Odontochelys* from the late Triassic of China. It had only evolved a shell on its underside. This suggests that turtles evolved as water-living animals. A shell on its underside would have protected it against the bed of a river or lake. It has long been a puzzle whether the water living turtles or the land-living tortoises evolved first. This discovery is one of the current lines of evidence that suggest the former.

A two-headed swimming reptile from the early Cretaceous was found in China in 2006. It was an abnormality. Every other specimen from the aquatic lizard-like *Hyphalosaurus* so far found has only one head.

Dakosaurus, a gigantic sea crocodile nicknamed "Godzilla," was found in Patagonia in rocks of early Cretaceous age. It was 13 feet (4 m) long and, whereas most sea crocodiles were obviously fish eaters, this had a skull like that of a meat-eating dinosaur.

There have been a small number of fossils of mosasaurs (*see pages 30–31*) discovered recently that show traces of the animals' skin. These show that they were covered with small diamond-shaped overlapping scales, like those of a snake, keeled on the top of the animal and smooth on the bottom. This suggests that they may have ambushed their prey by coming up on it from underneath—the rough surface given by the keeled scales would have helped to camouflage it from above.

Fossil mosasaurs have been found in Canada and Africa in freshwater sediments. It may be that, toward the end of the Cretaceous, they began to move into river mouths and deltas and take over the hunting grounds of crocodiles and alligators.

Recent studies have confirmed that plesiosaurs swam like sea lions. The front flippers could not be lifted above the horizontal, and the power stroke was the down stroke as the flipper was rotated. This is implied by the spaces in the skeleton that would have held the muscles.

Devonian rocks have always revealed monster invertebrates. The biggest so far was found in 2007, when the claw of an 8 foot (2.4 m) long water scorpion was found in Germany.

Some mosasaur specimens have been found that have a slight downturn at the end of the tail. This suggests that in life there was a fluke, like that of a primitive ichthyosaur.

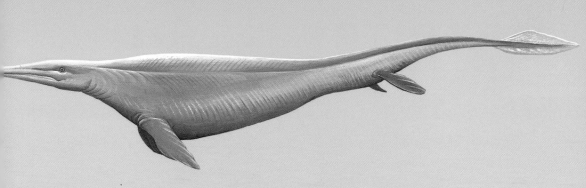

Stomach stones in the skeleton of the elasmosaur *Styxosaurus* found in Kansas consisted of rocks that only outcropped 373 miles (600 km) away at the time. This can only mean that the animal was able to swim over long distances.

The largest eye on record is that of an ichthyosaur. It measured 10 inches (264 mm) across and belonged to the ichthyosaur *Temnodontosaurus*.

Fossils of baby mosasaurs have been found in areas that were at least 200 miles (322 km) from the nearest land at the time. This shows that the females must have given birth to live young at sea, and did not come ashore to lay eggs.

There was a family of marine crocodiles, the dyrosaurids, that thrived in late Cretaceous seas, but survived the great extinction and went on to dominate the oceans in early Tertiary times.

It has been estimated that the big ichthyosaurs could dive to depths of 2000 feet (610 m) and remain submerged for 20 minutes.

The Triassic long-necked swimming reptile *Dinocephalosaurus* had expandable ribs in its neck. As it lunged at fish the neck expanded, sucking water in and drawing the fish in as well.

The disease called "the bends" affects divers if they surface too fast. Bubbles of nitrogen form in the blood and can cause paralysis. This happened to plesiosaurs, too. We can tell from damage seen in the fossil bones.

WEBSITES & FURTHER READING

WEBSITES

Wikipedia tends to be distrusted by many people because it is too easy to put spurious information on it. However, the dinosaur material published there is quite reliable and up to date.

www.dinosaursociety.com

All sorts of information on dinosaurs, including a valuable frequently updated page giving links to all the dinosaur-related news stories.

www.sciencedaily.com/news/fossils_ruins/dinosaurs/

A catalog of the dinosaur stories run by this news site.

Warning! *The articles presented by these sites are usually written by journalists, not by dinosaur specialists. As a result they tend to be over-sensational or sometimes plain wrong. If you find an interesting dinosaur news story it is a good idea to chase it up through different sources, to see how the story differs. Usually you can tell how much is fact and how much has been made up by the reporter. That's fun, too!*

There are more technical sites:

www.oceansofkansas.com

A site that keeps up to date with the research being done in the late Cretaceous marine fossils of the mid-west.

www.ucmp.berkeley.edu

This does a very scholarly review of current ichthyosaur research.

www.plesiosaur.com

A serious review of plesiosaur research.

Google Earth

Key in LYME REGIS. Here you will see the coastline of southern England where the first famous discoveries of fossil sea reptiles were made, and where Mary Anning worked (*see page 25*). Note the stepped appearance of the cliffs at each side of the town. They are constantly sliding into the sea and exposing new rocks and revealing new fossils.

Key in HOLZMADEN to look for the famous ichthyosaur locality in southern Germany (*see page 29*). You will see the town but not much else—the quarry closed years ago. But now key in DOTTERNHAUSEN and you will be taken to another site to the south-west. The huge quarry to the west of the town is cut into the same beds as the classic ones at Holzmaden and is producing the same kinds of fossils. There is an excellent museum in the factory complex just next to it.

Key in LOGAN COUNTY KANSAS. This is the area in which the first specimens of the sea reptiles of the Cretaceous inland sea were found, back in the 1870s. Flowing west to east across the county is the Smoky Hill River, and you can see the steep sides of the river with the rock strata exposed. Now key in CHALK BUTES, MANVILLE and it will move you to an area in Wyoming in which the same chalk rocks outcrop, and you will see them nicely as buttes and cliffs. This whole area—Kansas, Wyoming, Nebraska—was covered in a shallow shelf sea in late Cretaceous times.

Key in *57 15.81 N 123 00.92 W*. These are the coordinates of the site of the giant ichthyosaur from British Columbia, Canada (*see page 27*). Just look at the terrain in which the paleontologists had to work!

FURTHER READING

THE DINOSAURIA

Edited by David B. Weishampel, Peter Dodson and Halszka Osmólska, 2nd edition 2004

This is the bible for paleontologists. However, it is extremely technical and hardly to be recommended for the casual reader. And, since the science is constantly changing, the 2nd edition may well be out of date already.

PREHISTORIC TIMES

A quarterly magazine, running since 1993, features articles on dinosaur research and dinosaur lore. See their website **www.prehistorictimes.com**

A JOURNEY TO THE CENTER OF THE EARTH
Verne, Jules

Several English language versions since 1871. This features the description of a fight between an ichthyosaur and a plesiosaur, the first ever committed to paper in a work of fiction.

GLOSSARY

Algae Simple plants including the seaweeds.

Ammonite A relative of the squid and octopus, with a coiled shell, that lived in Mesozoic times.

Articulation The way one bone moves as it joins to another.

Belemnite A relative of the squid, with a bullet-shaped internal shell, that lived in Mesozoic times.

Carboniferous The period of geological time from 354 to 290 million years ago. The time of the coal forests.

Champsosaur One of a group of crocodile-like animals that lived in late Cretaceous and early Tertiary times.

Continental drift The movement of the continents across the surface of the earth throughout geological time. It is caused by the movements of plate tectonics.

Cretaceous The period of geological time from 144 to 65 million years ago. The last of the three dinosaur periods.

Desmostylian One of a group of hippopotamus-like marine mammals from the Tertiary.

Devonian The period of geological time from 416 to 359 million years ago. This saw the first flourishing of life on land.

Dyrosaurid One of a group of marine crocodiles that lived from the end of the Cretaceous to the beginning of the Tertiary.

Elasmosaur One of a group of plesiosaurs—the ones with long necks.

Evolve To change from one type of animal to another over generations, in response to changing condition.

Flipper A limb that has evolved into a broad flat shape to help in swimming.

Fossilize To turn to stone. An organism becomes fossilized when its organic material changes to mineral material after being buried for a long time in rock.

Gastrolith A stone held in the digestive system of some birds and dinosaurs, to help to grind up food, or in some sea animals to adjust the ballast.

Godzilla A fictitious movie monster originating in Japan in the 1950s.

Hyperdactyly The condition of having more than the usual number of fingers or toes.

Hyperphalangy The condition of having more than the usual number of bones in the finger or the toe.

Ichthyosaur One of a group of fish-shaped marine reptiles from the first half of the Mesozoic.

Jurassic The period of geological time between 206 and 144 million years ago. The heyday of the dinosaurs.

Mammal A warm-blooded animal, usually covered in fur, that gives birth to live offspring and suckles its young.

Mesozoic The era of geological time encompassing the Triassic, Jurassic, and Cretaceous periods.

Migration The movement of animals from one area to another, usually to new feeding grounds.

Mosasaur One of a group of swimming lizards from the end of the Cretaceous period.

Paleontologist A scientist who studies paleontology.

Paleontology (Spelled 'palaeontology' in Europe) The study of the life of the past.

Pangaea The name given to the supercontinent that existed in Permian and Triassic times, that incorporated all the landmasses of the globe.

Permian The period of geological time from 290 to 248 million years ago. Reptiles were dominant on the land but the dinosaurs had not yet evolved.

Phytosaur One of a group of crocodile-like animals from the Triassic period.

Plate tectonics The movement of the surface of the Earth driven by deep convection currents, which produces new crust all the time and gives rise to continental drift.

Plesiosaur One of a group of swimming reptiles of the Mesozoic, with paddle-like limbs and long necks or heads.

Pliosaur One of a group of plesiosaurs—the one with short necks and long heads.

Predator An animal that hunts other animals.

Prehistoric From before human history.

Pterosaur One of a group of flying reptiles related to the dinosaurs.

Prey Animals that are hunted and eaten by other animals.

Reptile A cold-blooded animal that reproduces by laying eggs, and is usually covered by a scaly skin. Lizards and snakes are typical modern reptiles.

Scavenger A carnivore that eats meat from animals that are already dead.

Sclerotic ring A ring of bones found in the eyes of some creatures, such as birds and ichthyosaurs.

Shelf sea A sea formed as water spreads over the surface of a continent, as opposed to an ocean, which lies between the continents.

Stagnant Of water, having not enough oxygen to support life.

Stegosaur One of a group of dinosaurs with plates and spines on their backs.

Tertiary The period of geological time between 65 million and 1.8 million years ago. It is the age of mammals and lasts until the last ice age.

Theory A selection of ideas that can be tested scientifically.

Triassic The period of geological time between 248 and 206 million years ago, that saw the beginning of the age of dinosaurs.

Vertebrae The bones of the neck, back, and tail.

INDEX

ACKNOWLEDGMENTS

The original publisher would like to thank Advocate, Helen Wire, www.fossilfinds.com, and Elizabeth Wiggans for their assistance.

Picture Credits: t=top, b=bottom, c=center, l=left, r=right
Lisa Alderson: 7b, 10-11c, 19t, 20–21c, 26–27c, 32c. John Alston: 6b, 10tl, 11r, 12b, 13br, 15t, 20t, 22l, 23t, 27t, 28l, 28b, 30t. BBC Natural History Unit: 7tr, 13t, 14tl, 17cr, 30cr, 33b. 35t. Corbis: 15b, 30b. Steve Etches: 16tl. Fossil Finds: 10b, 24t, 30cl. Simon Mendez: 6c, 12–13c, 14–15c, 18–19c, 23cr, 23br, 28–29, 28–30c, 32b, 34–35c. Natural History Museum: 18t, 21t, 26b, 29t, 33bc, 34cl. Bob Nicholls: 16–17c. Peterborough Museum: 17b. Luis Rey: 12t, 22–23c, 32–33c, 34t. Royal Tyrell Museum: 27cr. Science Photo Library: 20b. University of Bristol: 25b. University of Toronto: 6t.

Every effort has been made to trace the copyright holders, and we apologize in advance for any unintentional errors or omissions.

NOTE TO READERS